Not Guilty

poems by

Amatan Noor

Finishing Line Press
Georgetown, Kentucky

Not Guilty

For those hanging by a thread

Copyright © 2023 by Amata Noor
ISBN 979-8-88838-336-0 First Edition
All rights reserved under International and Pan-American Copyright Conventions. No part of this book may be reproduced in any manner whatsoever without written permission from the publisher, except in the case of brief quotations embodied in critical articles and reviews.

ACKNOWLEDGMENTS

I am grateful to the journals that published some of my previous work, often first versions of them.

Dandelion Screams first appeared in *DIALOGIST* journal
Bengali Wedding first appeared in *Stone of Madness*

Publisher: Leah Huete de Maines
Editor: Christen Kincaid
Cover Art: Syeda Mahbub
Author Photo: Tamanna Islam
Cover Design: Elizabeth Maines McCleavy

Order online: www.finishinglinepress.com
also available on amazon.com

Author inquiries and mail orders:
Finishing Line Press
PO Box 1626
Georgetown, Kentucky 40324
USA

Table of Contents

Camry 1

Currency 3

Agave Amica 4

Grease 5

Not Guilty 6

Apparition 7

Ways to Break a Surveilled Body 9

Here is Your Samosa Literature 11

When I Said Marrakech 12

Love Letter from My Loneliness 14

Coasted 15

Golden 17

Gone. Running. 18

Home 20

Dandelion Screams 21

Shaheed 23

Garden 24

Torch 25

Tributary 27

Monet 29

Bengali Wedding 31

I Regret Nothing 32

Camry

> *"It was almost never about food. It was about Tony learning how to become a better person"* —David Chang on Anthony Bourdain

He says,
You could be a prickly person
and squeezes my hand gently
Our hands become two stress balls squeezing the other's harder
and harder with each reciprocated *I love you* before I take off for Lisbon.

I fume in disagreement the whole flight
Say *no* to every meal segmented in perfect, tiny squares
and not because
I am not hungry

What follows is a
Do Not Disturb sign on my hotel room door and
I close the blinds on anyone who loves me
Leave every conversation
I want to be
     missed like the carefree warmth of a summer day but
worry I have become humid air

    When Allah handed out hearts, they let me walk
    away with a second hand 1999 Toyota Camry in my chest–
    durable and somehow still running after many close calls,
    surfaces chipped beyond repair

    I enter potholes without hesitation of unrest
    Something of so little value should have nothing worth losing

        In the mid-nineties,
        Murders of crows cawed Dhaka into ruckus of life at sunrise
        The noise pollution deafened the sound of all chaos by night
        including the boom of explosives detonating below the rickshaw
        next to my family and My Toyota Camry heart

        convinced itself to take the fault for the
        bodies at the core of a city inflamed in political turmoil and
        no one took the load off its trunk of guilt

What Allah forgot was to offload trauma from the parents so they remember to parent
and their children do not collect shrapnel
in their psyche for years to come

Sometimes I wonder if the loose shrapnel
are the prickly parts that get in
the way of my
love

When I was four,
I kicked the doctor during chemo
because it hurt
but also because he
dared think he could be causing me

pain

When I was seven
one lone crow came in through
the kitchen window every day
like a bad omen
and I did not chase it away.
It is clear now,
we were both unwanted and
therefore wanted by one another

Sometimes, I hang onto all that I love by the prickly parts
Sometimes, I hang on by so little

Currency

I question how civilizations conformed to the concept of money. Yes, I am aware of history and how bartering must have derived to be an improbable way to function and how we phased out metal and found better and much worse uses of them. Some say, *time is money*. What if time literally were money? And how much money we have was predicated on how much time we have spent not thinking about money but existing. The liveliest of journeys meet the most elusive of desires.

Once, my cousin and I ate kulfi out of a perplexing green banana leaf that unveiled refreshing sweets cool to the touch, midsummer scorching through our frocks onto skin.

The kulfi we exchanged for a pile of old newspapers from a man who carried a scale balance on his shoulders and shouted *Paper!* as he roamed around town. I am convinced this man was the God of serotonin, vanishing newspapers as part of a spell through which he emptied grief from the psyche of humankind.

With this new currency, every time I am given a sour mango masked sugary in a jaggery-soaked marinate, I spend a bunch to sweeten the tartness and the mango becomes a pulsating red and yellow with hues of orange and its juices drip down the corners of my mouth. From its juice the wrinkles around my lips transform to a half circle of a perpetual smile line and extract a liquid so sweet it earns me my first toothache but I am so happy I laugh uncontrollably.

I wonder if I can survive on laughter alone so the cow I once witnessed lie down for its own slaughter without protest prances like a gazelle back into the forest of its own continuation.

Whenever I am cold, I wrap myself in a banana leaf, and use the currency of life to bring my cousin back from the dead and we are once again eating kulfi wrapped in banana leaves safeguarded from all evils, our bodies cocooned by the sole carrier of joyful existence—banana leaf.

Agave Amica

I struggled to comprehend why I am nowhere to be found
in my parents' wedding video
As a child,
I rewound the cassette tape with a pencil
Heard Sabina Yasmin's voice set a ritualistic backdrop
Watched each scene incessantly like a frantic bird
to catch a glimpse of my younger self
perhaps missed in a blink as swift as a seagull after a french fry
There, my young, timid parents were
My mother adorned in tuberoses and marigolds from head-to-toe
An identical embellishment to the car that whisked them away
Someone must have taken me, I thought.
How else could I had been forgotten on the most celebratory occasion?
The first time my mother found
me stuffing my face full of grapes in secret
she made me regurgitate every last bit
and I listened with resistance, contempt even
The oncologist told us I could not eat any fruits with skin
Forbiddance only added to my yearning like a sweltering silver blaze
Amma miscarried the first time she was pregnant
The second time, she was finishing
her master's degree in botany with me in her belly
when bouts of morning sickness charged her body
like a swarm of bees before lectures
She, too, learned to dispose from the body
and go on pretending like the world is spinning as destined
I am almost certain my mother learned of tuberoses in her botany lab
memorized its scientific name using an index card
I cherish an old photo of her unmarried self in a field of tuberoses
her mouth wide open from laughter's exuberance
inhaling youth's fragrance, a cloud of tuberose scent
In that place she is an uncut stem
There is a place where she imagined using her degree
There is a place where she is not left to clean
the communal bathroom of an entire
children's cancer ward
so that it is hygienic for my use

Grease

"*We daily forgive the bourgeoisie*" —Tongo Eisen-Martin

I am a keeper of strangers' possessions
On the night summer breeze drank jaggery spiked with rum,
the smell of moonlight let me dig a tunnel from my vision to
the touch of a kerosene lamp–

hotter than the taste of a village beating!

I am dreaming of a leg of lamb but first,
let me oil myself up and swim across
my conscience and none of this is on a
whim

I have planned this since the last time the moon looked like
my pocket watch
and fought with the sun over custody of all planets
but earth

Even though I drink moon juice everyday,
I want to avoid all its shine when I mistakenly keep my neighbor's television
I splattered his goat with sunflower oil and it's slippery to the touch
put a muzzle over my mouth
You know–

recipe for the greatest heist of our generation

Once I die, my butler will
trickle down one six-ninths of my wealth
thirty decades later

Not Guilty

[~~Thanksgiving~~] weekend, instead of gorging on game by the plateful, I frantically swallow fear in the form of questioning from prosecution as I prepare for a trial I awaited four years. I was sexually assaulted during a neurological check-up. This, an hour before the internet led me to account the defense attorney had been a felon convicted of firing warning shots at a woman he once loved, once held captive as she found escape leaping out of a two-story window. *I didn't want to kill the woman,* he said. Fractured heels were the imposition on the victim and a shortened sentence was of the assailant. A shortened sentence and a law degree would later cross our paths. A man once convicted on charges of violence on a woman's body was reformed and positioned to vet the validity of violence women's bodies the same year I was born. This, the court of law permitted. And long before this, the law permitted medical insurance companies to afford denial of care to women listing rape and sexual violence as preexisting conditions. This rule had been revoked shortly before my perpetrator would be found not guilty on six victims' claims. So when given the opportunity to ask any questions before I embark on this path, I crumble into exhaustion, let the path fold before me and do not bother. Instead, I answer all the questions asked of me. My upbringing's demand of indubitable obedience since childhood was partially to blame. Perhaps, it could be fathomed, in that moment, I had known no court of law was set up to serve me justice, the kind of law where men allow for men's beguilement and men help men plead *not guilty.*

Apparition

[Defense Attorney: Are you familiar with the concept of implanted memory, Ms Noor?
Judge: I see the direction you're going in; overruled
Defense Attorney: You must agree your memory today is less accurate than what it used to be three years ago. How valid is your testimony today, Ms. Noor?]

Motionless, she laid still in an attempt to scream
but her throat let out only shudders of horror in muffled rackets

Amma called her sleep paralysis the mute
However, she was the *mute's* embodiment

She awoke escaping fever dreams claiming,
a couple more seconds, and I swear I would have died

I am told all the pain in our dreams is scripted by our own subconscious
all faces constructed from faces known all along—a motion picture of horror
for the motionless

    In my dreams, I am being r[aping]ed by men of [un]known faces
    Their images hunting the crux of my conscious as I combat my way
    to an escape
    mouth—*a mute* like my mother's
    body—frozen like an icicle on the coldest day of frost

The tale of two bodies in toil are lost memories
of ways we become prey and
[our bodies]
freeze like permafrost below the surface
when our mouths are hushed with fists, and bayonets, and shame
    [our bodies]
    shapeshift from crime scenes
    into war zones and collaterals
    We know to burn the abuse
    into the backs of our skulls
    to pass along to
        [our bodies]
    and the bodies of the ones
    who come after as caution

One body is East Pakistan revolting itself into Bangladesh
One Marches in the streets of Dhaka decades later to liberate

[our bodies]

One body tells the attorney
I need a minute because I am triggered
No. I will not look at you nor the defendant
(I like to pretend the demons are strangers in the nightmares that keep me fighting for breath)

We preserve refuge in this collective ache
never had the luxury to forget
We remember rape camps*
the bodies taken
the bodies gone
the pain that lingers without language
There, too, was coercion back then
to deny us our suffering
by those who were our assailants

We manifest a fable of horror and hallucination
but our bodies remind us the truth
We must etch the violence onto our limbs
Live its numbness in a cycle that is infinite
We cannot heal
from what is still happening
This trance of trauma
we must endure

*During the Bangladeshi Liberation War of 1971, thousands of Bengali women were abducted and held captive in barracks, where they were raped incessantly for months. Many died due to inhumane conditions.

Ways to Break a Surveilled Body

You move faster now
The hurt is in the background but always on the burner
The day you traveled from one coast of Turkey to another at dawn,
you felt less than courageous
Survival thrusted you forward like exhaust
The gray sunrise of Antalya spelled *unwelcome* on the horizon when she sent
chills into the marrow of your bones
So did the TSA agent at JFK when he wouldn't let you board the plane unless you
gave him the location of your stay
This used
to be more startling back in the day.
   In Vienna, when the policemen followed you into the train,
     they were surprised at the
        blue of your American passport
          They could have cared less about the
             blue you felt

Your frail heart let out sad sighs and
untamed tears the entire ride
You did not ask for this
        Not the glances that follow
          the laser that infiltrates more than body
          the scars and blood from the blue-eyed boy
          in Munich—he called you beautiful
There is an anticipated malaise that comes along with
patted down top knots
and waiting long past your check-in to watch others
[unlike you]
pass by with their dignity intact
The vindication is not desired but
treasured

You haven't been happy and
start to show little acts of defiance
unnoticed by everyone but you
You no longer wear a bra to the airport
The bitterness on your tongue is a dagger
to your four white girl friends after spring break in Cancun
where you were told to remove your shirt
at the gate before departure with
no divider to hide the humiliation

                                    and they don't bat an eye

You are apathetic, discontent at the museum
where they paint the president a hero
You stare at the unerring detail to the
shadow of his wedding band
while the distant, dead children of
sand who became smoke from
the drones he struck remain faceless

You and Maryam* speak half-heartedly after her
CNN interview with a pro-Palestine stance
You both agree she must be under surveillance
and therefore she might as well speak her truth
Besides, there are many ways to break a surveilled body
            (The ghost of "war on terror"
            sweeps like a feather in the heavy
            air)
You shudder as you recall all of them

*Name altered to protect surveilled body

Here is Your Samosa Literature

Hyperpigmentation etches roadmaps from both corners of my lip to my chin
liberates countries under my eyes that I look to decimate like the west waging war
with costly chemical concoctions in pretentious, tiny jars

I see Brown women carry maps of neighboring cities on their faces and they stretch wide as we exchange laughter and conspire in weed smoke exhaling toxic patriarchy from relaxed vessels

We cry in unison at our prowess and I am certain the blueprints of our faces combined would encircle a globe we would palm like dough rolled by ancestors they transformed with vigor into

sustenance

When I Said Marrakech

I meant the stars not buried in skyscrapers
To you it was the scrape of a distant boyhood
I guess I still search for the child in me to heal
You love Manhattan more than you like to admit
Your eyes are a nighttime skyline of brightness
when your mouth is full of cityspeak

We embrace envisioning a Morocco that splits us apart

Marrakech meant the stillness of us in bustling glimmer
surfing palms until we locked fingers
Instead, we hold hands on makeshift Brooklyn hilltops
You twirl me around wishing oblivion
land me on the cliff your chest
absorbed in the waves of your heartbeat
I forget my own

Pray an avalanche so love becomes maktoub
Each bead on the the tasbih is a bone of your rib I try to move closer to mine
Dhikr reminds me your tenacity is a mountain I'm trapped under
And matters of troubled hearts seldom move mountains

Faith is a silly topic we circle when it does not keep us kind nor together
        but circling past one another

We try to make this love holier than hellish
You call me *habibi* only in bed

Each breath of *Bismillah* you exhale is a blasphemy
Utter God a thousand times
Your eyes still scream starvation; not ask

We are in hunger with each other all winter

I want to soak in every last drop of this spring
I am on the closest brink   of departure
even if it means self-destruction

I'm on a bicycle headed to facelessness
I'm a bicycle with no breaks nor handlebars
I'm the bicycle's back wheel drained of all its air

The wheel is my sinking heart

And my punctured heart lets out broken sighs
and huffs and puffs of anger mid-deflation
but turns around for one last glance
hoping you do the
same

Love Letter from My Loneliness

all of brooklyn is ethically non-monogamous,
to pull off this stint, i wear a different colored cloak each week to drape us both in
i know you crave the waist grip of a whirlwind-romanced dip,
but you are rawest when we sway to rhythms
sequenced by sweetness of summer breeze and
dry prosecco you were meant to wane off downing
a polychromatic confetti of falling leaves i bequeathed you in october
they match the bronze under your sunken, sleepless eyes

i emptied the streets and cobbled them with jeweled symmetry for us to peruse all winter

don't push me away.
you think i am the deadly, bitter snowstorm
i just happened to be the only one who clung onto you like a cold breeze
don't say i treat you like an estranged lover
i light the forgotten candles next to the klonopin
and latex-free condoms you prefer to keep hidden
cradle you like a newborn after all departures i saw coming from miles away
nurse the bruises on your breasts from men who never loved you

beg you this time to stay a while longer

Coasted

San Francisco shows me
Hilltop homelessness somehow protects the city's chic
Yet she haphazardly packs the burdensome
like worthless trinkets bagged for disposal
Says,

>*You have no home but you can't stay here*

I know this city sleeps despite all its glint
The hungry try their hardest
Steep slants of a smug San Francisco will stare back at you with no repentance
The view is stunning and
                gutting [   ] with callous apathy
It extracts everything human -
logic, compassion and history of a once unwavering revolution

In San Francisco,
Monument of a man
folds to his most mortal form—

>*I am dying from the inside, he says*
>*But I will not go down without a fight*

He grabs his mortality by its throat everyday and
Suddenly, the strife of San Francisco becomes him
Suddenly, I keep him on my pedestal
a little while longer

He says there is calm in the Pacific ocean
Says in the Atlantic,
he can still see the blood spilled in transatlantic captures
and I believe him in a heartbeat
But after the unrelenting waves of the Pacific
leave me with
scraped knees and a fear of drowning,
I am left to ponder

>*Don't all oceans trick us by*
>*feigning calm and enchanting a clear blue?*

They pull us in and to teach only some of us survival

I want to tell him,

> *No ocean has ever kept afloat our kindred*
> *They have voyaged those who*
> *drowned us for centuries one way or another*
> *But we are the lucky ones, you and I*
> *to be in hazy aftermath*
> *comparing the atrocities of oceans from afar*
> *fortunate to be parted by something other than water*
> *drowning not at sea, but in one another*

Golden

Where do I find a love that rivals yours?
I told the forest your name
to find its worthy opponent
It echoed back the same
When I turned to sea it became salt
Each grain a dried up tear drop
When I looked to the sky it cleared blue
crossed a thought so clouded
crossed my mind even

Love,
when stars shine
Light bends onto earth
Just as my spirit zigzags to your warmth
My eyes see nothing but stars
Our bodies collide
I tremble all over
I looked at the Sun
She said,
    Bask in this warmth, because you, my darling, are golden

Gone. Running.

Once I leave
the path breaks out into a
clavicle branching into a shoulder like
a twig protruding through
an air conditioning unit
I will not trim
I want to see the unfolding in both
I have learned
it is better to observe
the unraveling of a dirt road
than to be the roadkill
splayed on its damp surface
by an intruder of the body
If you see me now
you may be right to assume
I am suffering the misfortune
of an asthma attack
but I have gone running
against my lack of athletic acumen

Feet, do not trail the mud
of the hidden grassy puddles
We are heavy from
carrying the brunt of
a body broken down like cardboard
after it once hauled gifts

Hands, do not forget
to swing when the leg below you has thwarted
We.Can.Never.Stop.

Fingers, curl as if you were holding a potato chip
between each index finger and thumb
that no force of agony will crumble
like the weight of self-blame

Mouth, do not eat the potato chip
We are on a mission to forget the
taste of anything that leads to danger

Mind, wander into the gates of lazy, lilac thrills
for this momentary torturous pleasure burst
a runner high so euphoric
it could bring an unicorn to climax

Soul, do not return
For I have promised you
I will aid in your escape from all that is achy
for as long as I can physically swallow this scalding porridge
the monster continues to pour down my throat

Home

I am not here to paint some kind of false narrative. We were not inseparable at birth. You were my cousin on my mother's side. Her brother's daughter and one year older so we got lumped together often. There were times I didn't like you either—like the day you pulled down my pants when I was taking in the barrage of monsoon by the window and in vengeance I chased you for hours after because I wanted to pull your pants down too. You knew how much I loved the rain for its deluge of plenty. We scrounged up change from our parents' pockets and hopped on rickshaws and when it rained, pulled back their hoods and looked up at the clouds so the showers land right onto our faces. We went from rice paddies to railroad tracks cloaked in false invincibility until my mother and one of our grumpy aunts chased us down, scolding us for stolen freedoms and wet hair. You always took the brunt of all punishments.

I took so much from you —the sleeping spot on the bed, the bigger piece of meat, the ripe fruit, —but you never complained. It was how we perceived life. Unfair and granted. My daddy had more money and a temper and yours had left when you were a small girl and made sparse and sporadic phone calls. But we didn't let that stop us from extracting all the juices of girlhood. How those in charge despised the squeals our laughter let out like a jingle celebrating a kinship they could never have, telling us we were too young to close the door and talk up a storm or leave the house alone as if we would ever listen

***

It is monsoon again. I take a leap. I meet a man. He tells me he has heard of overpopulation in Dhaka caused by tragic flooding in its outskirts and mispronounces Dhaka about a dozen times. We drink overpriced cocktails while he blames the floods on Exxon. He never calls me back. Though comically excruciating, this is what I wish you could have suffered; whimsical ignorance of white folks masquerading as romantic endeavors. Not death by the way of childbirth. I think about how easily it should have been me if only Allah had swapped our fathers. I try to cover up my guilt in all kinds of ways. I send money to your toddler and newborn who are now motherless and don't yet know who I am or what money is, really. I tell myself it is not my fault that I could not keep in touch. Our families squabbled like packs of wolves over land and money and food or anything else that they were convinced was worth a damn.

> Deep down, I know what I am most guilty of. It is greeting every monsoon with a cheerful embrace and leaving it to you to pull me out of muddy waters with a tight grip while your universe had been engulfed by the menace of flood.

Dandelion Screams

It is all kicks and no scream, this
August
Rubbles lodge at my throat and
I prepare for new deposits with half a smile
Erupting rashes days after he left,
I self-soothe my body with
aloe vera and
Klonopin that is losing tranquil in
its prescribed dose
The rashes are from stress and not
estrangement; this I am sure of
I am trying. I pick fresh mint but
wake too fatigued to make the tea
blow on heads of dandelions
wishing he changed his mind
watch bees caress white clovers on
overgrown grass at
Fort Greene Park
Wonder if they mourn loss of
precious time pollinating the things
no one marvels at
Secretly, I wish each clover is a
lover the bees took in the early
spring
Say a prayer for a love that tender
When the reds on my body
mushroom into restlessness,
I urinate on pregnancy tests in four
different public restrooms and
heave until all of me flare into a siren
The child I would have rid my
belly of
It is the scorching heat, the culprit;
not his scorched-earth exit
He is not to blame
The bad men I know
perpetuate harm by
kicking down doors and
their screams leave behind a
wreckage
They make their presence

known
How could he be at fault?
At his most wrongful,
he was silent
At his most thoughtless,
he is absent

Shaheed

I've got belly bloated confidence   there is rage in my veins
boiling into hatred   fighting for a just undoing
backed by a violent police state   intruders will be due for comeuppance
militarizing land   prisoners will be taken after
the bullet becomes a mirror of   shrapnels splattered after a rightful war waged,
freedoms granted through occupation   of bodies and borders drawn with bootstraps

I will make a foreigner out of you on land that has always belonged to me

Garden

> *"Even hate begins to feel like love because there is at least acknowledgement"*—Jerrod Carmichael

Amma says this life is not worth dying alone
So I dig a grave inside my body to die a little bit everyday
    She says to
        fill my body up with budding offsprings,
        softly whispering motherhood into belly

If tenderness is a blanket,
I felt it wrap around me like calming lavender
when a beloved offered me laxative tea from Vietnam—
My mental state debilitating from gaining *pandemic weight*

The grave inside me absorbs each tea drop
like the drought of a clean kitchen sink
From its fractures beetles rush, scattering brown
They prod my thighs into cellulite caves

When fear is swaddled in lonesome aches,
I pause riding into the perfect sunset
Bring Theo a granola parfait
Put sunny, yellow tofu from my plate onto my lover's
Take from their plate what I crave

The Portuguese riviera trails my lone feet,
its waves as turquoise as Chinatown jade
They rain a monsoon on my grave

    A poppy grows on my head

Torch

you both arrive at the fish market
of silver and pearly glaze
after his failed attempts of
unhooking his fingers from
your stubborn ones
with empty bait

the fishmonger reels in a loud laughter
from him that is an unfamiliar tide
floats the freshest, flapping fish
and guts it before you

the gutting is a familiar firelight in your belly
like the firelight of your clothes
he will once set ablaze
you will believe
you deserve it

you take heed
his temperament
is a boiling tsunami
when the fishmonger swims
with caution between laughter
and bargain and banter

you cling to the wave of silence
because the empathy he has
for the way you feel
the world in a glut
is the size is of
 a fish
  eye

you begin to envy the fish
he knows to tend to
albeit before
slashing
its gill

after you no longer eat fish for a decade
and cast forlorn spells to dive at the

bottom of alcohol bottles and
into beds of wrong lovers
for affection

and when the stars begin to shed
like fork-tender fish and fall from a
mid-autumn sky you
wish for a revival—
scales propagating
on a bed of lilies

at the sight of his favorite fish, you freeze
docile, like a slug on levitating stem
as he fishes for credit, for love, for ownership
You must painfully acknowledge—

My father could have been a better man

Tributary

Like no president is a savior
you are not a pretty plunge basin
Where does this self-inflicted
crushing, copper weight of obligation come from
where you surrender to wither the waterfall in all of its selfish gliding descent?

You avoided softness from the balm of girls' hands
soup spooned grief out of the photo and
into your body to serve to slurping mouths of salivating men

This body hasn't belonged to me since my rustiest memories. I am not generous but disbanded

You don't like to drink alcohol but you like to sit in it
this ashy, graphite masochism of guilt and rot
and you like to believe there lies your respite

My self-loathing has nowhere to go so it festers into a cactus and pricks me when I settle into rest

One moment
you were uninhibited
a soundtrack of laughter caught in affectionate limbs
after a trustful toss off the balcony

One moment
Your mother placed your toddler body on her vanity like an ornament
Next, the Padma river engulfed your uncle
but your mother hasn't swallowed her grief since
You watched her wail into the maze of days passing while his body remained unfound
You did not save the almond candy he left you as goodbye
See, there you go plummeting down the tunnel of self blame
You were four and not one privy to premonitions of capsizing paddle steamers
Padma overflowed every monsoon, a haven of watershed and land erosion
And how could anyone keep away from her?
The way she enticed us all with kaleidoscopic glimmers of hilsa fish,
Synchronous orchestras of hawker's chants

Back then, no one called it a catastrophe—
                    this displacement of murderous water
at the expense of tawny people across the globe

Monet

When the splattered water lilies
washing onto the wide walls of a rectangle room
leave you rattled
Their precise painted brush strokes are akin to the
sweat of panic forming on the pores of your cheeks
It is the hasty wanderer in you that will want to escape your body
It will want to leave the museum past the curved bridge and
the chilly stream of flowing river
and the oceans and cities you traversed to ask yourself,

If I could be removed from my dread, shrouded in drab, dismal fog of blundered past
will I find safety in this broken body?

But remember—
you have always shifted the weight of colossal dread
from one oblique of crooked trails
of your body to another despite the
location of escape
because the body you are born into is one
that is clawing itself out of the coffin of toil
in perpetuity
And if he had been found guilty of
all his sins in the small town that you
seldom set foot in
and if all the women he had cleft from
blossoming out of his practice
bloomed into a garden
how would you cultivate
the fruits of your misgivings in
a world that would rather
see you rotten?
Would you believe with the
green moss of certainty that all the
women who walk
alongside you know to say
the name of the fruit you
choose to bear?

Think about cleaving
Let it be a fire

Let the fear of
disintegrating in its flame into
soot and silt
creep into your excess
the folds of your
belly and the roots of your hair
I now know why you are
clenched like a sparring fist
We are all
all smoke in the face of
the salacious

Perhaps no flower will make you
giddy today and
perhaps you are afraid to
let yourself soak into the
fabric of why that is

And if we are all bodies
cleft of the asylum
that houses reprieve

then

let us look over our shoulders past the backs of our
necks where every hair follicle stands up to thick
pungent scents that violence emits
past the bridge that leads to the
waterlilies
past the train and
wombs and oceans
until we have no place
to look but back into
the soft fertile
valley
of our
own
chest

Bengali Wedding

The groom's family had not asked for dowry in the traditional sense
Their demand was not of land or a motorcycle—
Some decent clothing, furniture, and jewelry for the bride
and a nice meal for the wedding guests
Partition left Bengal in unfair, impoverished halves and my grandfather penniless with too many
daughters to marry off
So when his second daughter's dead body surfaced floating on a pond in her husband's village
a year after a disreputable wedding unmet of demands and unfed guests
The village whispers buzzed, before the pond, the body hung from a wooden panel on the ceiling
Before that, the body was heard screaming
Before that, the body regretted its birth
Before its birth, the body that birthed the body
hoped it will have a better life devoid of pain
When I ask my mother if she has any regrets in the way she raised me
She says coming *here*
She says it pushed me away from her and Abba
and I wonder had we stayed if
I would have been just another body
shuddering myself asleep
feigning contentment at learned obedience for a chance at survival
waiting for my body's turn to be squashed under one man's thumb from another

I Regret Nothing
after Hanif Abdurraqib

& there are days when it is still 2018 & I follow the prosecutor's instructions & pack two fast-fashion turtlenecks to look of *good moral character* & hop aboard a Greyhound bus to Atlantic City filled with gamblers looking to flip their fortunes as they would to the cleaner side of a soiled couch cushion.

I try to suppress flashbacks of private investigators knocking on the door of my family's home with the force of earthquakes hauling boulders. I feel no pity for myself upon realizing ringing eardrums can fall silent when a criminal trial comes knocking nor that no one will join me in the courtroom nor that I have to stay at some discount hotel a five-minute drive away from my home affixed to a diner courtesy to the State of New Jersey.

I am given three meal vouchers to said diner for two nights to satiate any inkling of hunger and part of me believes if I deserve *this*, I deserve nothing less. I sit on the hotel bed & gorge on french fries after the diner staff cast a net to extrapolate gossip about some large trial many people had arrived in town for. Instead, I leave with my French fries returning no favors remorselessly. Next morning, I am escorted by two policemen too early for morning dew to form on leaves & both the prosecutor and I help ourselves to shiny, blue packets of Oreos for breakfast when our stomachs are two growling leopards springing in anger at a taunting fate & isn't it strange how our guts remind us there is an ocean of women who will wash ashore on this earth like prancing starfish hoping for a just world only to be emaciated by the Sun against hot sand?

Despite it all, I do not regret keeping faith as short-lived as a childhood.

Additional Acknowledgments

My deepest gratitude extends to you, beloved reader, for embarking on this narrative that was often coarse and wrinkled.

Survivors, I believe you. No questions asked. This book is for all of us.

I would like to thank my mother, the epitome of unconditional love, my father and my two younger brothers. It is with intention Allah has chosen to flock us together to wither the oscillation of joys and sorrows in this life. Through unconditional loyalty and dedication to one another, we persevere another day.

I stand on the sacrifices of my ancestors and relatives- some of whom have never left our villages in Bangladesh. May my storytelling honor their journeys.

I would like to thank Nafis, my sweet friend of childhood and Hanna, a kind, selfless soul who were integral parts of my resilience through the journey of survival.

I cannot grasp life's existence without the splendor of affection from friends and chosen family. Mandy and Sherry, thank you for being my first friends and chosen sisters who continue to support me while I remain too far away for too long. Chiamaka, James, Nizum, Sabah, Lorraine, Lindsay M, Victoria, Molly, Maggie, Trisha, Julianny, Aryanna, Tasnia, Omar, Alexis and Syeda- life can be mellifluous amid this siren of chaos due to your friendship.

Theo, thank you for walking into my life when I was shifting in and out of the discomfort of lack of belonging and making me feel welcome in any room. You saved me from the crippling loneliness propagated by this haunting mouth called New York City.

Thank you to Nuyorican Poets Cafe, Brooklyn Poetry Slam, SupaDupa Fresh, Emotional Historians, Kan Yama Kan and any other space that has allowed my work to grow. It genuinely takes a village and mine is a nurturing one.

My writing would not convert to something fruitful if it weren't for the caring, encouraging and supportive community of poets and writers in New York and beyond. I am fortunate to be in community with all of you. Thank you for making me feel celebrated and treasured.

Jive, thank you for being my rock in this space. There are not enough pages to express my gratitude. You made me feel worthy and seen when I had three poems to my name and never let me go. I cherish your kinship immensely. Mahogany, none of the spaces I walk into would exist without your legacy. Roya, you are the homie through and through. I don't know where I would be without your kindness. Hala, I love you so, so dearly and I look up to you as an older sister to cultivate my life with grit similar to yours. Noah Arhm Choi, Tongo Eisen Martin, Jon Sands, Rico Fredrick, Adam Falkner, Tarfia Faizullah, Phil Kaye, and Jeannan Verlee— thank you for your guidance and mentorship. I would like to thank Sara Deniz Akant, Dante Clark, Ayling Dominguez, Chanice Hughes Greenberg, CJ Parker, Lindsay Young, Ekoko Omadeke, Lyn "Paragraph" Robinson, Caroline Rothstein, Alesha Smith and countless others who have inspired me to continue writing.

Amatan is a Bangladeshi writer Based in Brooklyn, NY. She migrated to the United States in 2005 and spent her adolescence in New Jersey. Her poetry appears in DIALOGIST, Thimble, No, Dear and elsewhere. Her work has been nominated for a Pushcart prize. Amatan attended Rutgers University where she earned a dual Bachelor's degree in Information Technology and Sociology. She began her writing career partaking in poetry slams. Amatan has won poetry slams at the Brooklyn Poetry Slam and Nuyorican Poets Cafe. Over the course of her writing career, her work has evolved to explore themes of dislocation, physical and generational trauma, diaspora, Islam and the multitudes pertaining to womanhood. Amatan lives in Clinton Hill and is in an ongoing love affair with Fort Greene Park. *Not Guilty* is her debut collection.

www.ingramcontent.com/pod-product-compliance
Lightning Source LLC
Chambersburg PA
CBHW022044080426
42734CB00009B/1231